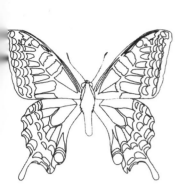
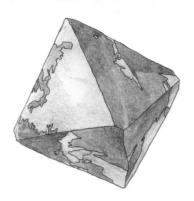

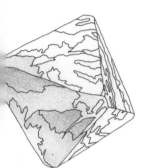

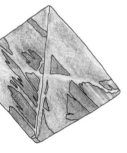

CURIOUS NATURE

COLORING JOURNAL

....

Color and Discover Fascinating Flora, Fauna & Fungi

RUCHKA

(Kayoko Sato & Satoko Sasaki)

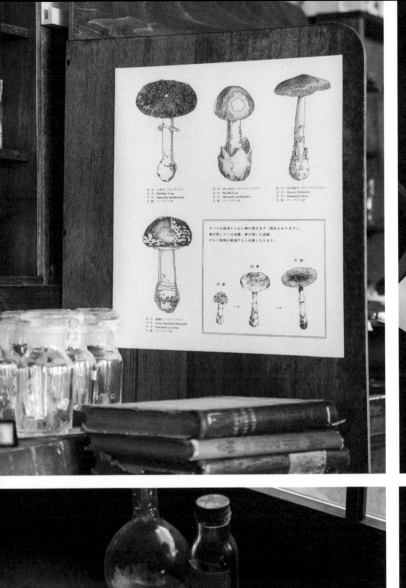

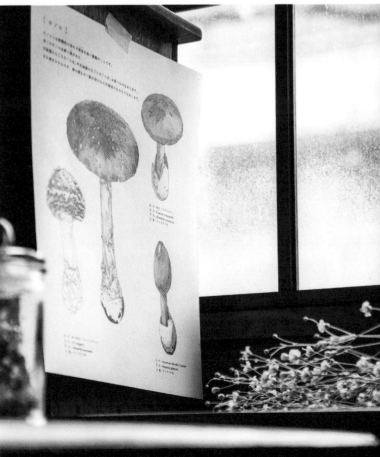

COLORING TECHNIQUES

The following guide contains helpful tips and tricks for coloring the different types of illustrations found in this book. Follow these steps to create realistic images, or just have fun creating colorful, one-of-a-kind illustrations inspired by your wildest imagination.

Minerals, Gemstones & Fossils

When coloring something as intricate as a mineral or gemstone, it may be helpful to study a reference photo. Photographs capture color, dimension, and shadow, which are important elements for creating a realistic illustration.

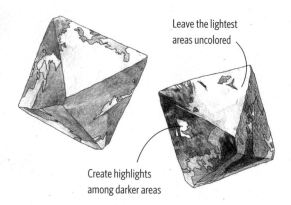

Leave the lightest areas uncolored

Create highlights among darker areas

When coloring a gemstone, think about the way the light hits, revealing the transparent nature of the stone. Leave the lightest areas uncolored, then surround those areas with lighter shades of the color you plan to use for the rest of the stone. To express highlights, leave one small spot uncolored in the middle of a darker area.

Metallic colored pencils can be helpful when trying to accurately reproduce minerals such as pyrite or galena. If you don't have a metallic version of the color you need, try layering gold or silver on top of a regular colored pencil.

Try adding fantasy-inspired designs to your illustrations for a mystical effect

Coloring doesn't always have to be realistic. You can create fantasy-inspired illustrations using images of the night sky, ocean, or geometric designs. Use your imagination...the sky is the limit!

How to Add Shadow

Try adding shadow to the illustrations for an even more realistic effect. When adding shadow to a transparent object, such as the crystal shown here, it's important to identify the location of the light source.

1

View of the image before it's been colored.

2

Start by shading the facets of the crystal that are not hit by the light source. Use the side of your pencil to add a faint ring on the left side.

3

Make most of the facets shaded in step 2 even darker. In this example, the darkest facets are located on the left side of the crystal.

4

Use the side of your pencil to make the ring even darker.

5

Make the facets and ring even darker. The ring should show gradation from light to dark as it spreads outward from the crystal.

Scientific Tools

Most of the scientific tools depicted in this book are made of clear glass. To capture the look of glass, leave a bit of space uncolored along the outline, then shade from dark to light. Use a darker color than the rest of the illustration when coloring the shadows. Think about where the light source is located and leave these areas uncolored for highlights. Have fun and make the illustrations your own by adding colorful liquids or interesting samples inside the glass jars.

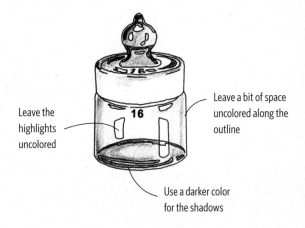

Leave the highlights uncolored

Leave a bit of space uncolored along the outline

16

Use a darker color for the shadows

Mushrooms

There are so many different varieties of mushrooms, each with unique features and color schemes. Look at photos and drawings for inspiration, or create your own one-of-a-kind mushroom using your favorite colors.

For a realistic look, use shading to create three-dimensional looking bumps on the cap. Use a slightly darker color to fill in the bottom half of each bump. Make sure the shadows are all coming from the same direction.

Use a darker color for bottom half of each bump

Butterflies

Butterfly specimens are often drawn from a back view to showcase the intricate wing designs. Follow the steps below to color the butterfly illustrations included in this book.

Start with the lightest color first. It's alright to color outside the lines as you will add darker colors on top later.

Next, fill in the patterned areas of the wings, including dots, stripes, and other markings.

Finally, fill in the veins. Many butterflies exhibit gradation with darker colors at the edges of the wings and lighter colors toward the center.

Tip

For butterflies that don't have a clearly defined wing pattern, layer similar colors to create subtle shading and gradations from light to dark. Fill in the veins to complete the illustration.

Acorns

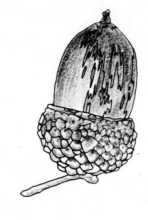

Acorns are light green when they're young, but they change to brown as they age. As with any object, use lighter colors for the parts of the acorn that are exposed to the light, and darker colors for the shadowed areas. If you only have a few colored pencils to work with, try applying a light layer of ocher, then add a layer of brown on top. You can achieve beautiful depth by layering shades of green and brown, even when working with just a few colored pencils

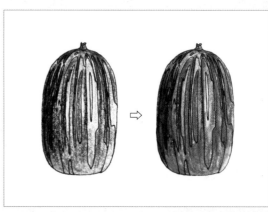

You can achieve beautiful, soft finishes working with watercolor pencils and a brush dipped in water.

Tip
You'll want to leave the highlights mostly white, but you can create a more realistic effect by softly shading the outline of the highlight. If you look closely, you can see light brown along the edges of the highlight.

Feathers

Most of the feathers included in this book are primary feathers, which are the main flight feathers on bird wings. These feathers grow outward, which is important to keep in mind when coloring. Always start from the shaft and color outward. If the feather is shown flattened (like in the example at right), use a slightly darker color for these areas and draw the lines with the sharp tip of the pencil.

Use heavier pressure to make these areas darker

Use lighter pressure at the ends

Start from shaft

Introduction

One of our favorite childhood memories involves visiting school over summer vacation to take care of the class' pet rabbits. After finishing up outside, we went looking for the science teacher in order to return the keys to the rabbit hutch. He was nowhere to be found, so we began exploring the science classroom.

Despite the summer heat, the classroom was cool and dark, and it felt as if time slowed down as soon as we stepped inside. The walls of the room were lined with shelves filled with all sorts of interesting specimens.

There were minerals of all different shapes and sizes, including a grayish-white druse that appeared as if it was filled with cotton balls. It was labeled okenite. I touched the fluffy white crystals and was surprised to find that they felt just like the rabbit I petted earlier! I grabbed my notebook and began sketching this unique crystal.

Colorful sea urchins and starfish lined the shelves of the marine specimen collection, but I was drawn to a strange object with six legs. It was sitting inside a box lined with cotton and labeled "Stephanocyathus spiniger." I copied down the name so that I could look it up at the library later.

There were also fossils, both of leaves and sea creatures. Some looked as if they had been stamped into rocks, while others looked exactly like modern specimens, as if they could come alive at any moment.

Then, all of a sudden, we heard a loud bang! Our science teacher appeared out of nowhere, as if by magic.

To this day, we still remember our time in the science classroom fondly. Inspired by the mystery and beauty of the minerals, mushrooms, fossils, feathers, and other specimens that we loved collecting and observing, we have created a coloring book full of unique illustrations for you to color. Our hope is that these illustrations bring back memories of days spent discovering and spark your creativity as you enjoy coloring these beautiful and curious objects of nature.

—Ruchka (Kayoko Sato & Satoko Sasaki)

Quartz

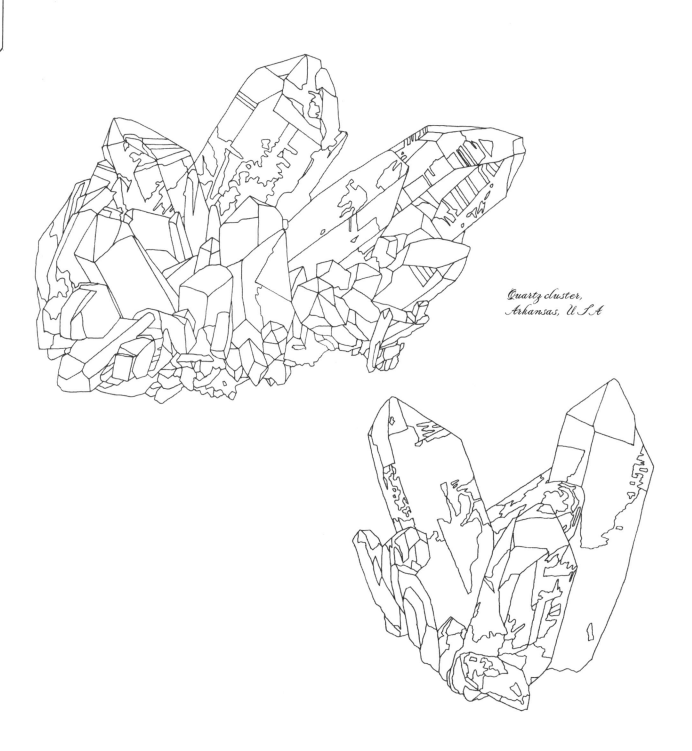

Quartz cluster,
Arkansas, U S A

Quartz cluster,
Arkansas, USA

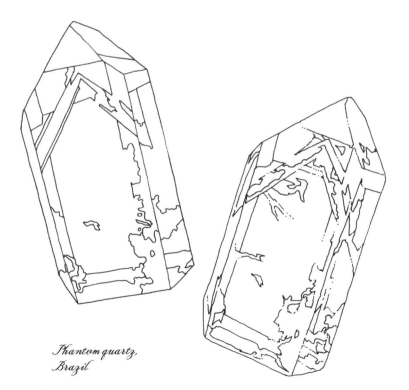

Phantom quartz,
Brazil

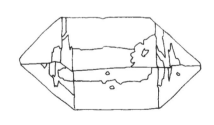

Herkimer diamond,
New York, USA

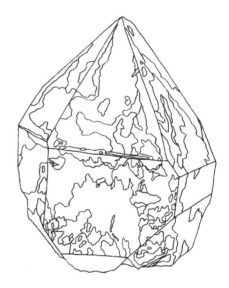

Amethyst, Uruguay

Amethyst, Morocco

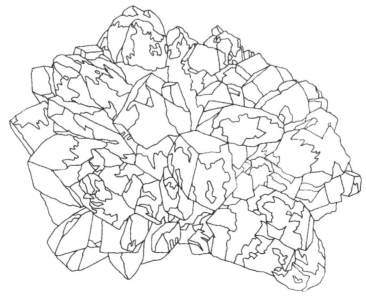

Amethyst, Brazil

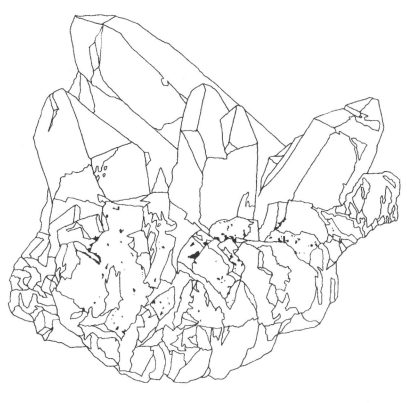

Smoky quartz, Brazil

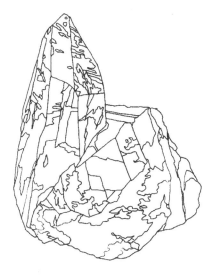

Citrine, Brazil

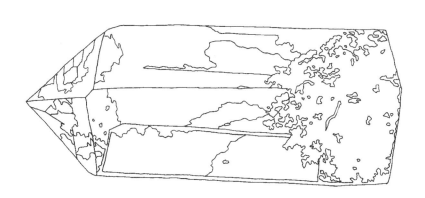

Garden quartz, Brazil

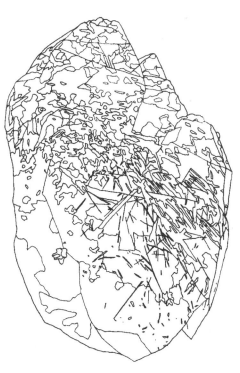

Blue quartz, Brazil

Fluorite

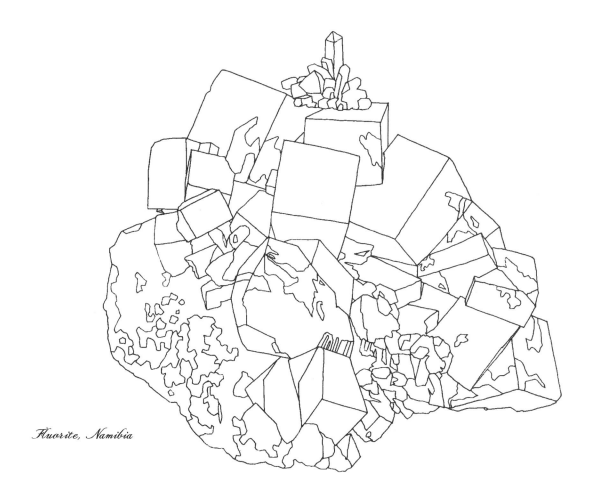

Fluorite, Namibia

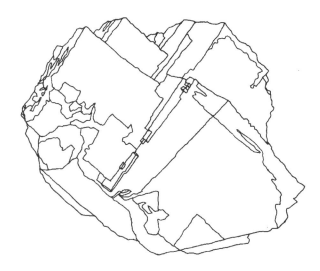

Fluorite, USA

What's in a Name?

The word "fluorescent" was coined in 1852, when George Gabriel Stokes examined specimens of fluorite and discovered that they produced a blue glow when illuminated with light.

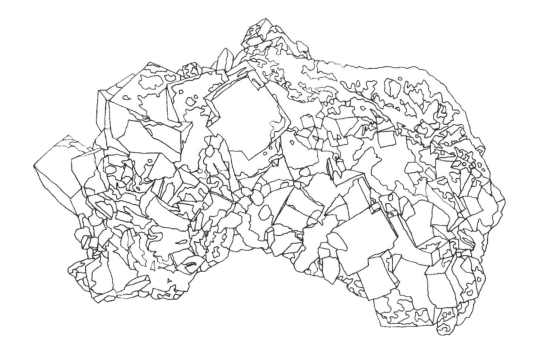

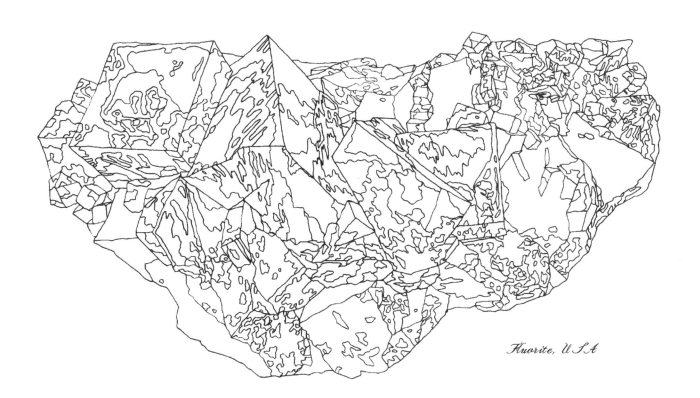

Fluorite, U.S.A

Fluorite octahedrons

Other Fluorescent Minerals

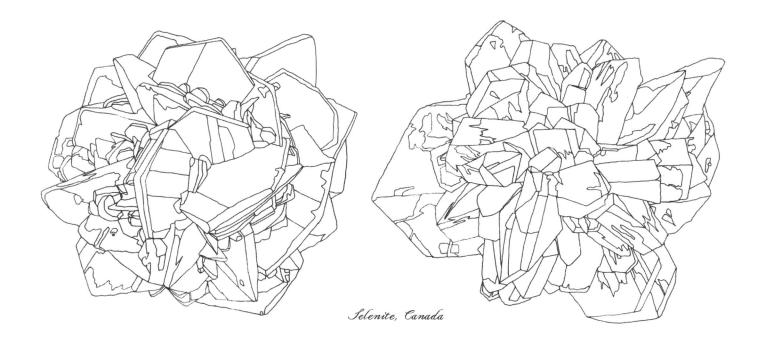

Selenite, Canada

Selenite, Germany

The Cave of Crystals

One of the most famous sources of selenite is the Cave of Crystals in Naica, Mexico. It contains giant selenite crystals that are larger than telephone poles!

Selenite (with hourglass fluorescence)

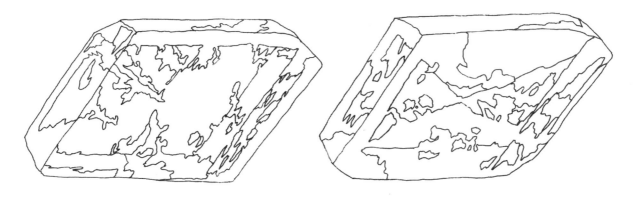

Normal   *Under UV Light*

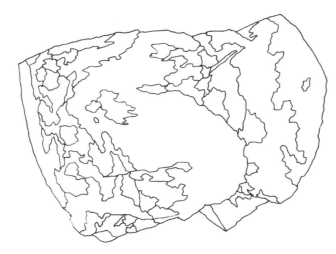

Hackmanite, Canada

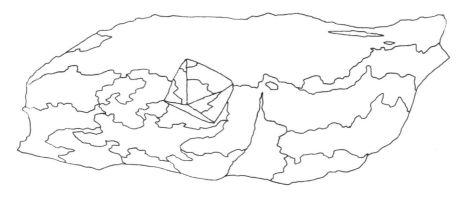

Spinel, Myanmar

Other Minerals

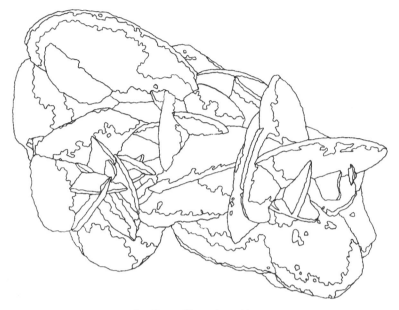

Sand rose (barite), Morocco

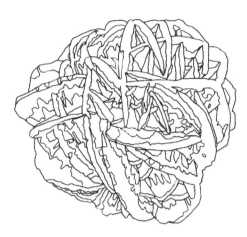

Sand rose (gypsum), Mexico

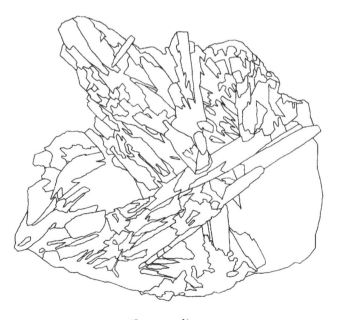

Barite, Morocco

Rosasite, Morocco

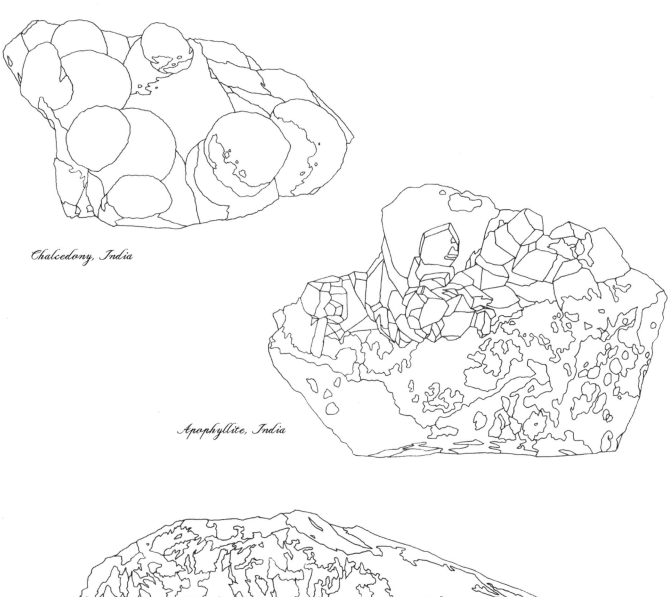

Chalcedony, India

Apophyllite, India

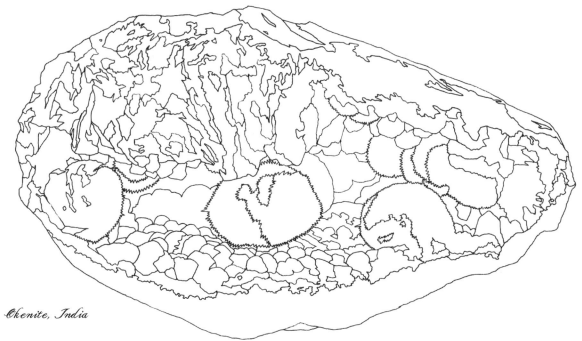

Okenite, India

Calcite, USA

Calcite, China

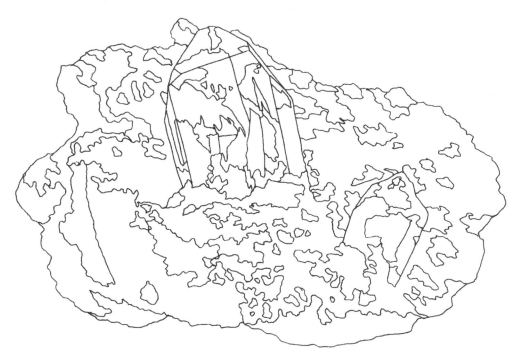

Topaz, USA

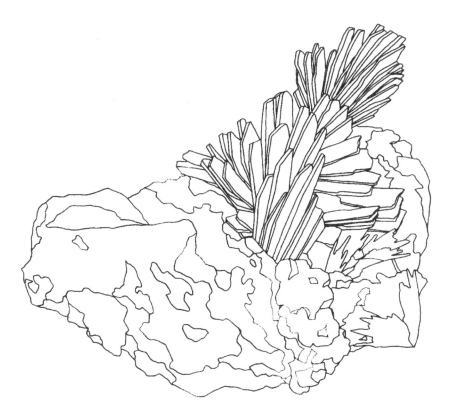

Hemimorphite, Mexico

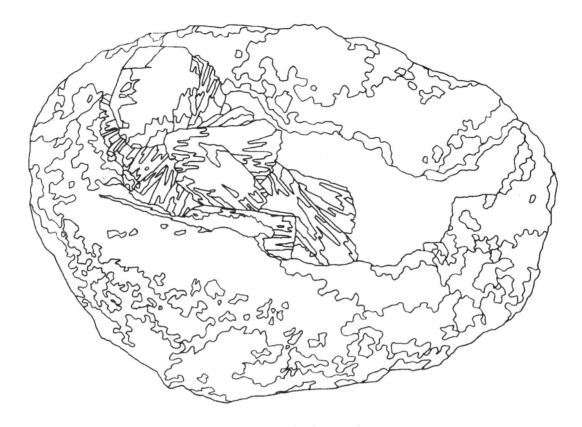

Heulandite, India

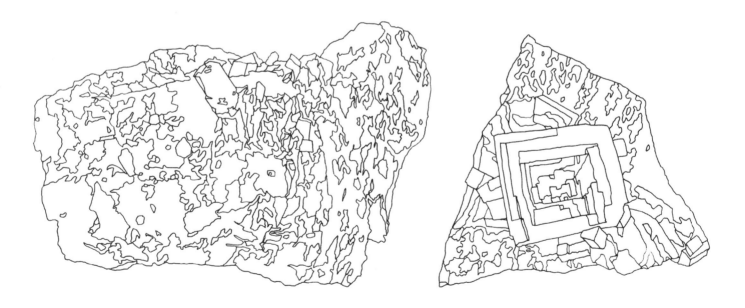

Neptunite and benitoite, USA

Halite, USA

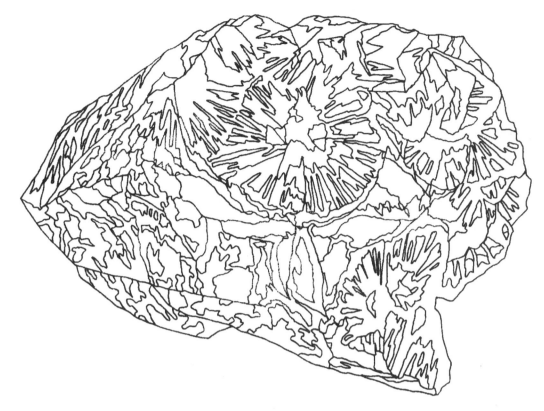

Wavellite, India

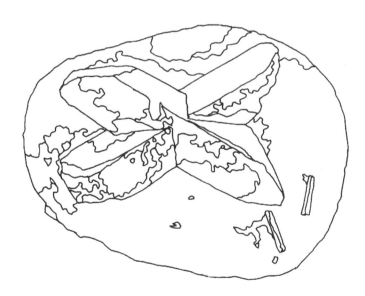

Staurolite, Russia

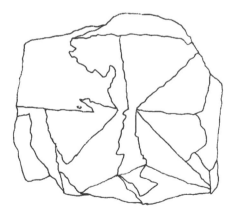

Staurolite, Madagascar

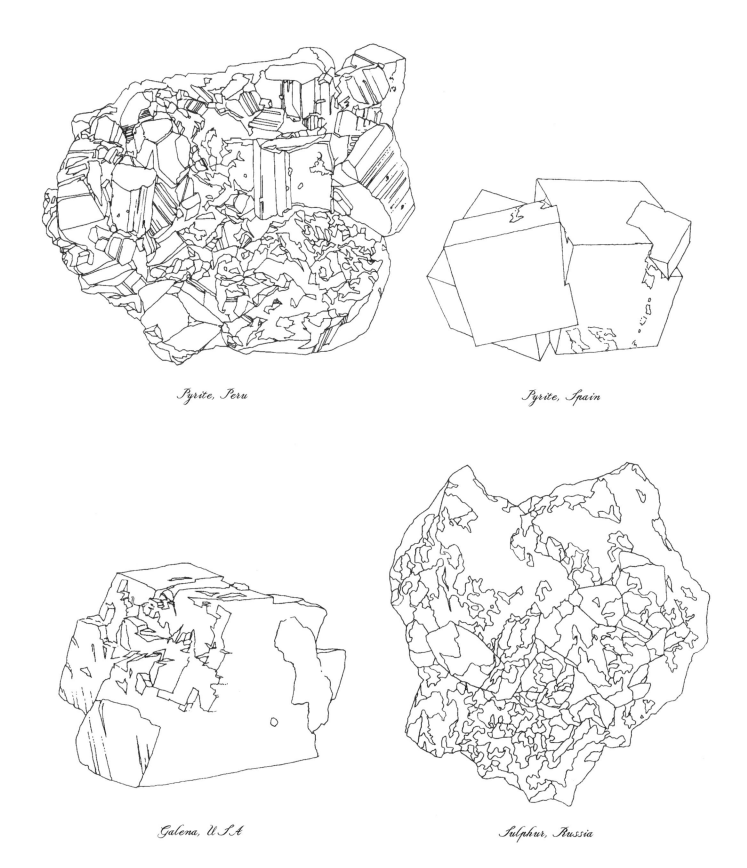

Pyrite, Peru

Pyrite, Spain

Galena, USA

Sulphur, Russia

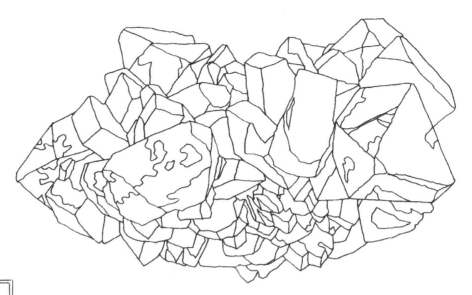

Celestite, Madagascar

You're a Gem

You may have heard of the gem aquamarine, which is the birthstone for the month of March. Aquamarine is actually a variety of beryl. Other gemstones that are varieties of beryl include emerald, heliodor, and morganite.

Beryl (aquamarine), Pakistan

Mica

Muscovite, Brazil

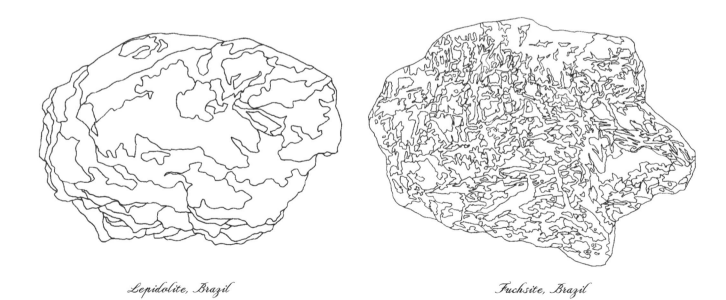

Lepidolite, Brazil

Fuchsite, Brazil

Ammonite

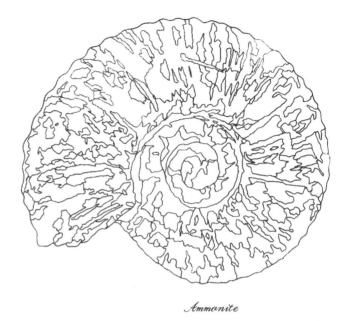

Ammonite

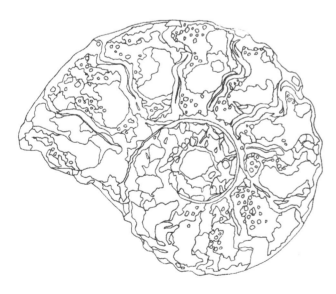

Inside view of pyrite ammonite

Inside view of ammonite

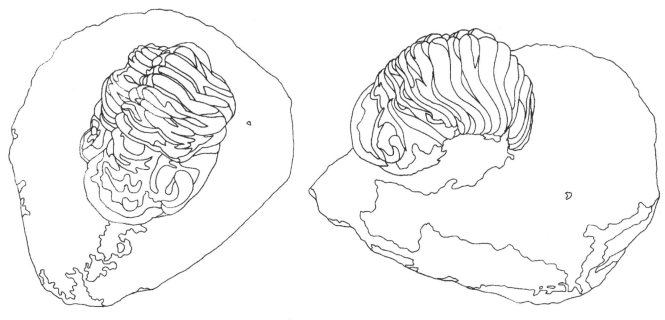

Trilobite

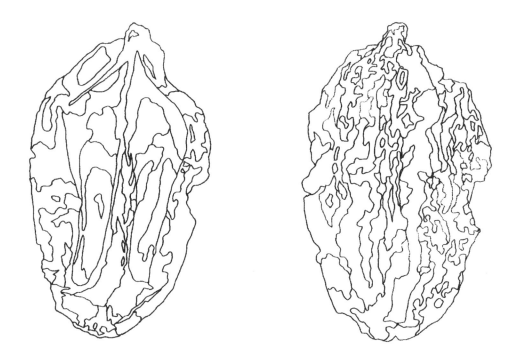

Butternut (white walnut)

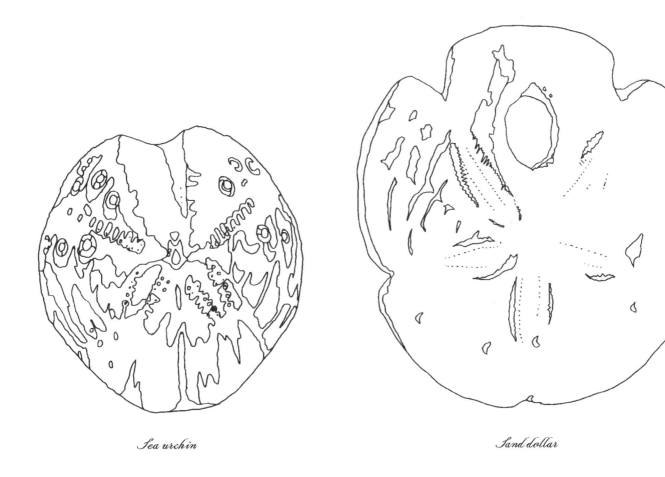

Sea urchin

Sand dollar

A Unique Stone

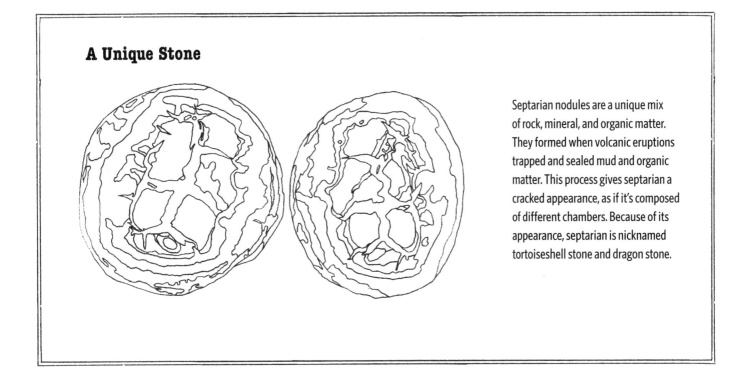

Septarian nodules are a unique mix of rock, mineral, and organic matter. They formed when volcanic eruptions trapped and sealed mud and organic matter. This process gives septarian a cracked appearance, as if it's composed of different chambers. Because of its appearance, septarian is nicknamed tortoiseshell stone and dragon stone.

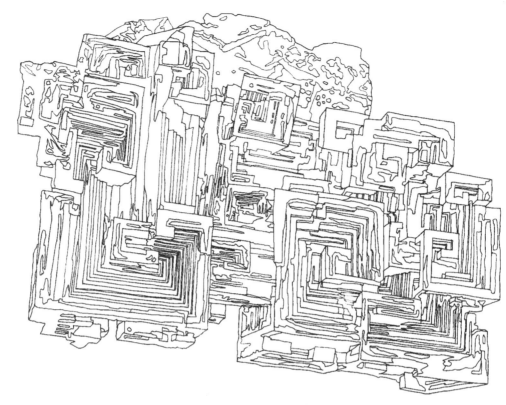

Bismuth

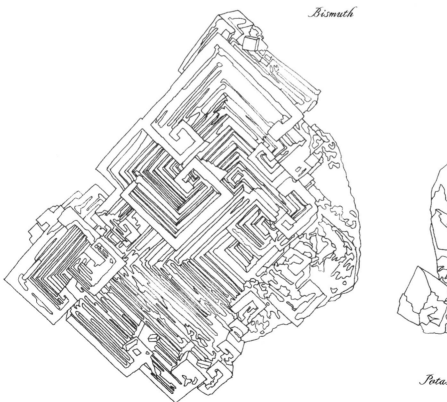

Potassium dihydrogen phosphate

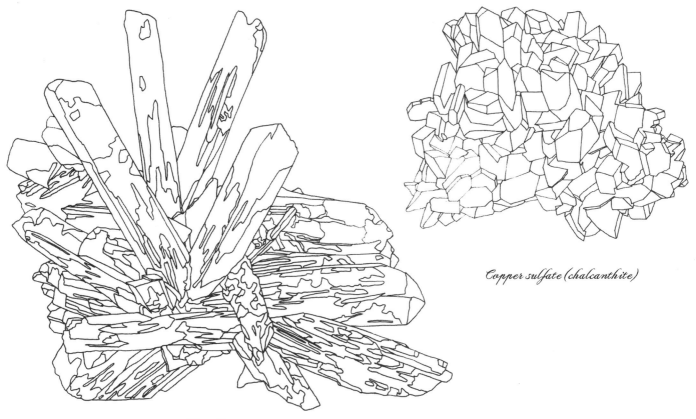

Phosphate

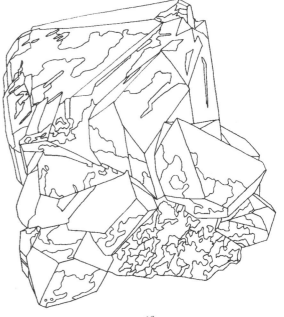

Copper sulfate (chalcanthite)

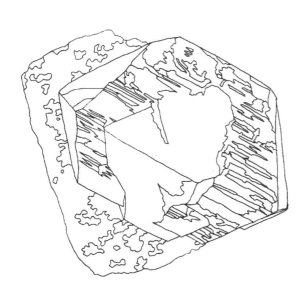

Potassium sulfate (arcanite)

Alum

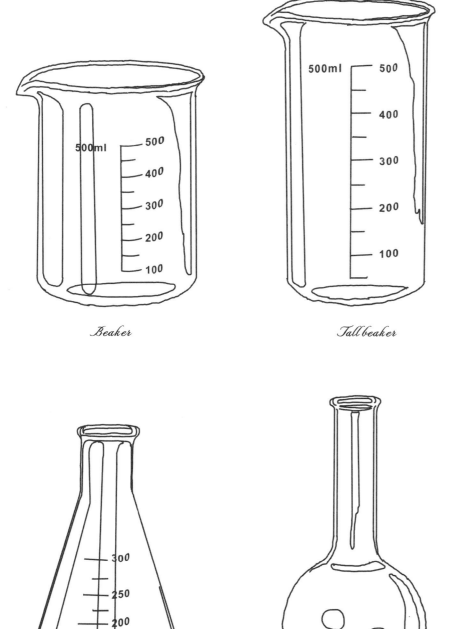
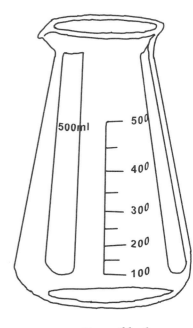
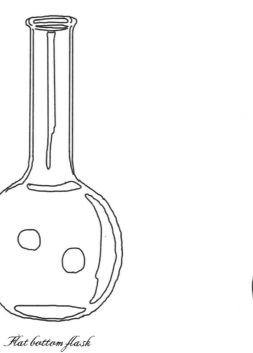

Beaker

Tall beaker

Conical beaker

Conical flask

Flat bottom flask

Volumetric flask

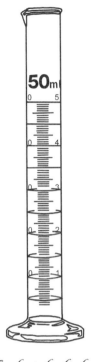

Graduated cylinder

Wide mouth reagent bottle

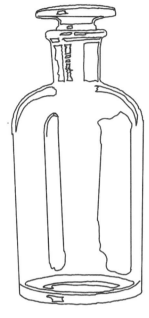

Narrow mouth reagent bottle

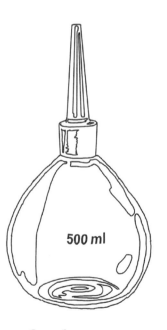

Gay-Lussac pycnometer

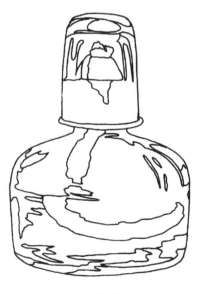

Alcohol lamp

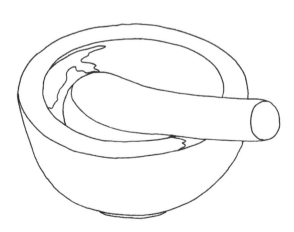

Mortar and pestle

Weighing bottle

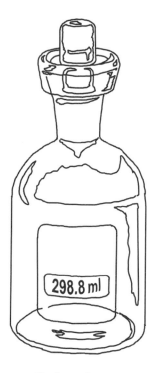

Biological oxygen demand bottle

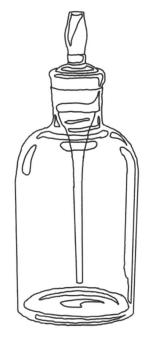

Dropper bottle

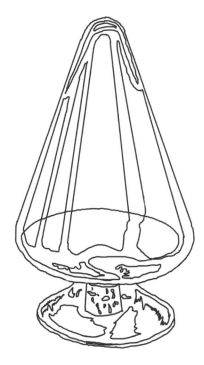

Seed flask (squid type)

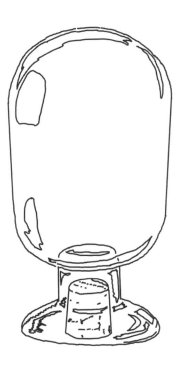

Seed flask (octopus type)

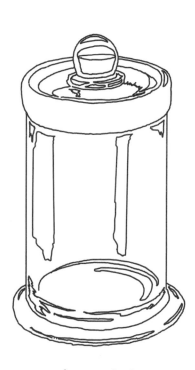

Specimen bottle

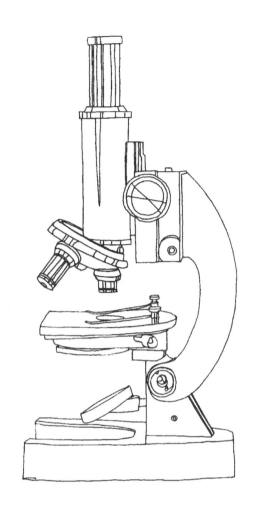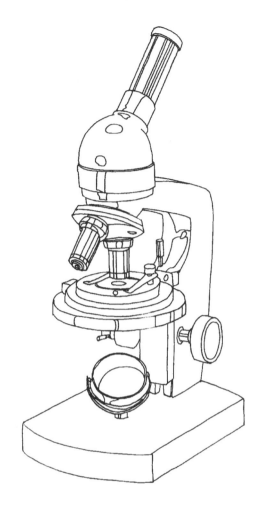

Microscopes

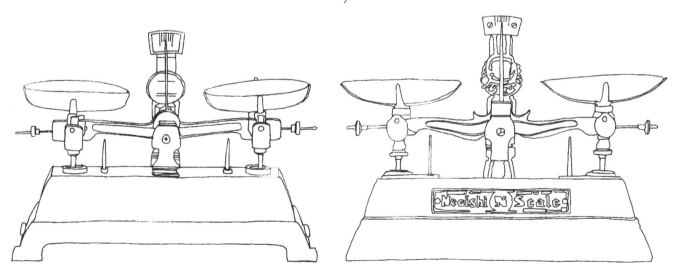

Double pan balance scales

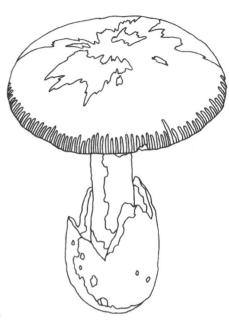

Half-dyed slender Caesar

Fly agaric

American slender Caesar

Panther cap

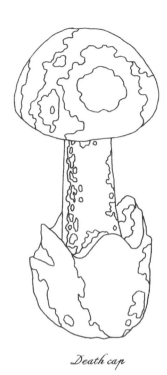

Death cap

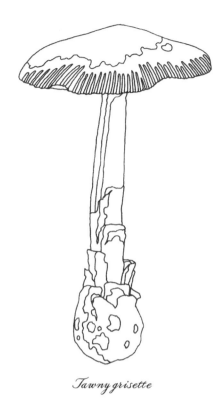

Tawny grisette

Grey spotted amanita

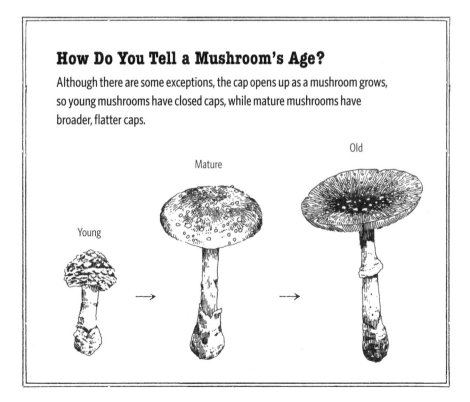

How Do You Tell a Mushroom's Age?

Although there are some exceptions, the cap opens up as a mushroom grows, so young mushrooms have closed caps, while mature mushrooms have broader, flatter caps.

Young

Mature

Old

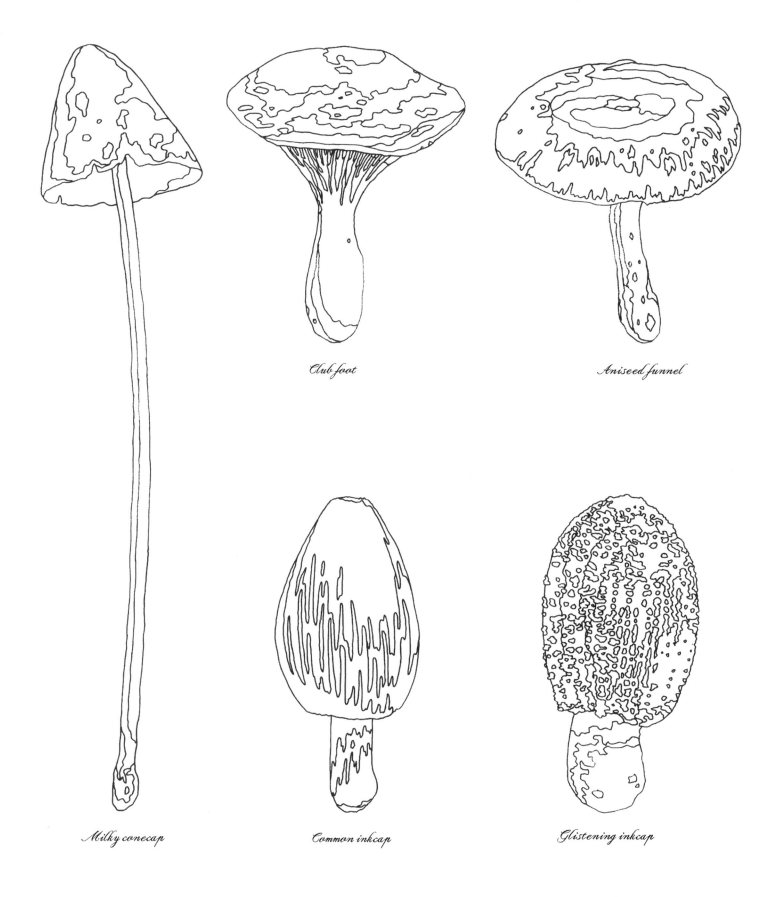

Club foot

Aniseed funnel

Milky conecap

Common inkcap

Glistening inkcap

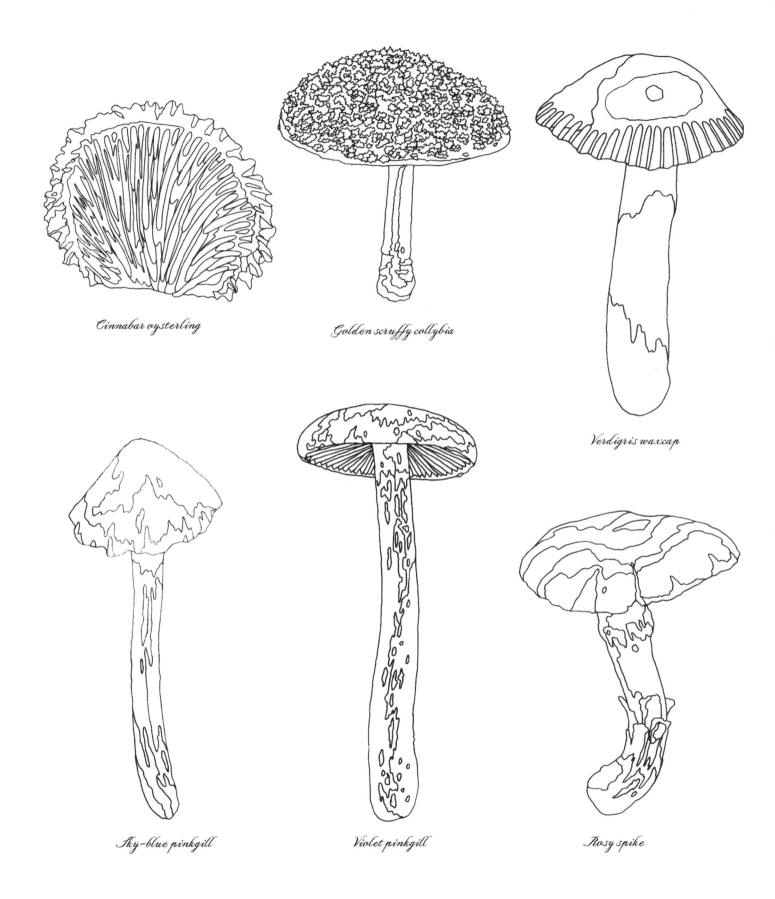

Cinnabar oysterling

Golden scruffy collybia

Verdigris waxcap

Sky-blue pinkgill

Violet pinkgill

Rosy spike

Russet toughshank

Pink waxcap

Shining waxcap

Magpie inkcap

Slender roundhead

Bloodred webcap

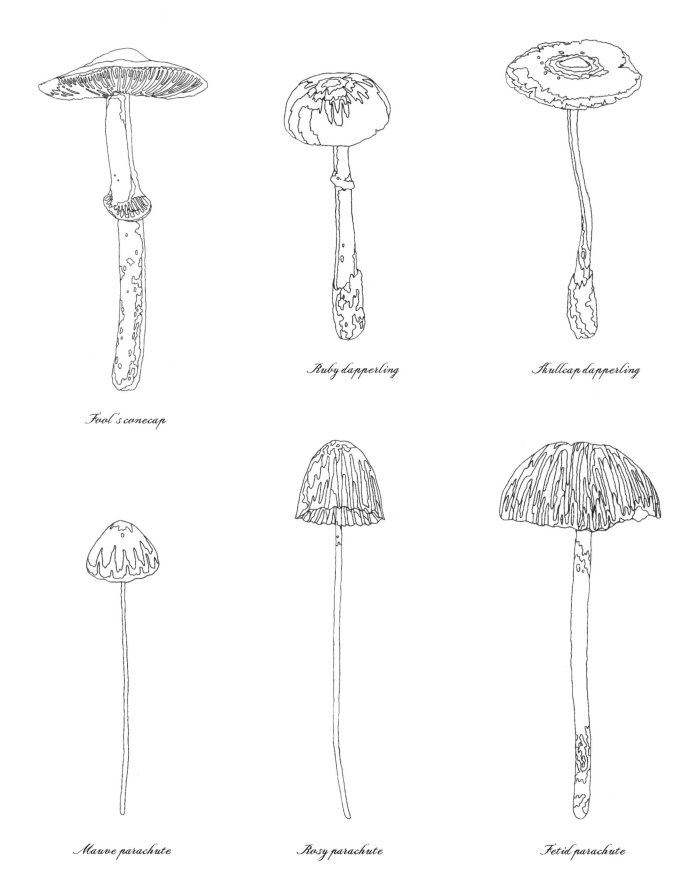

Ruby dapperling

Skullcap dapperling

Fool's conecap

Mauve parachute

Rosy parachute

Fetid parachute

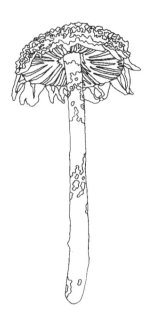

Redspored dapperling

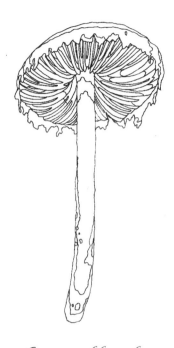

Greenspored dapperling

Scarlet bonnet

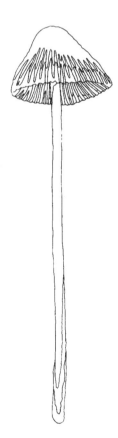

Tangerine bonnet

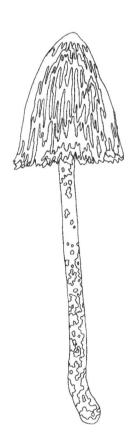

Bleeding bonnet

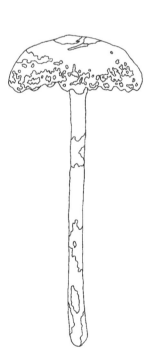

Ruby bonnet

Pixie's parasol

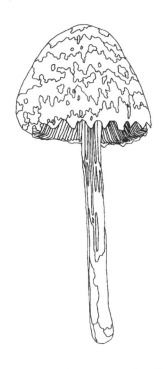

Petticoat mottlegill

Pleated inkcap

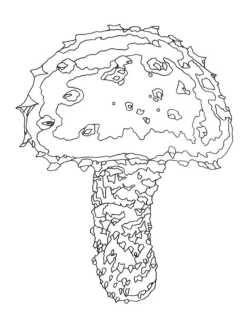

Golden scalycap

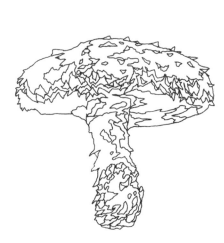

Flaming scalycap

Verdigris agaric

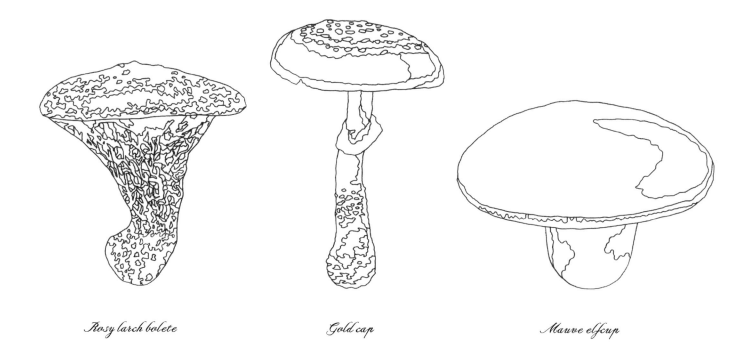

Rosy larch bolete   *Gold cap*   *Mauve elfcup*

Black velvet bolete   *Rhubarb bolete*   *Zeller's bolete*

Uniquely Shaped Mushrooms

Starfish fungus

Devil's fingers

Devil's tooth

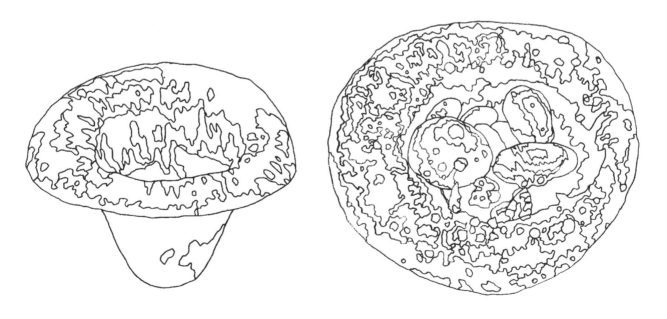

Bird's nest fungus

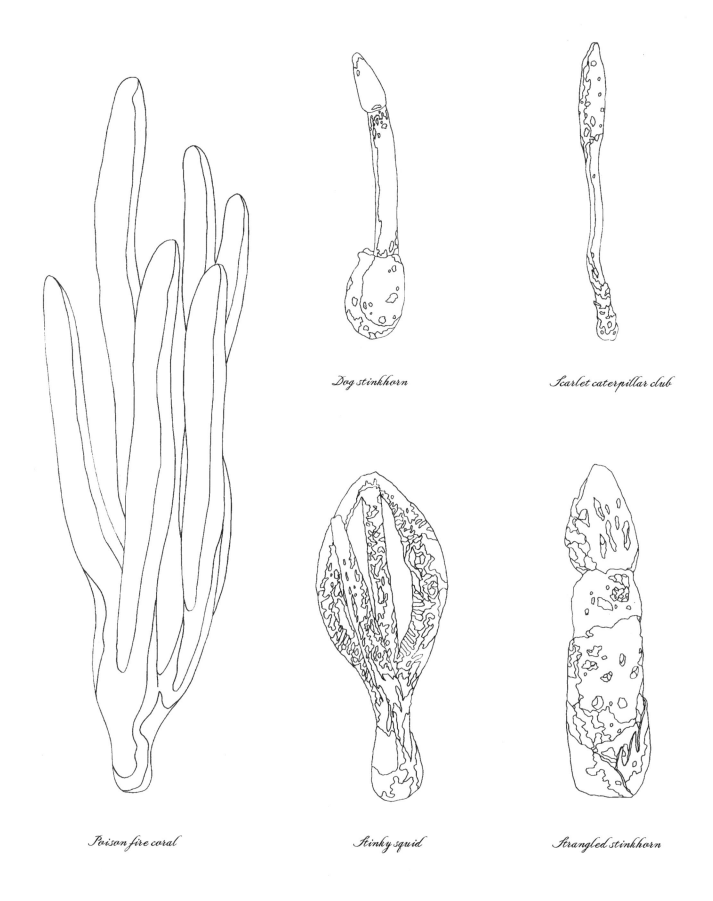

Poison fire coral

Dog stinkhorn

Scarlet caterpillar club

Stinky squid

Strangled stinkhorn

Collared earthstar

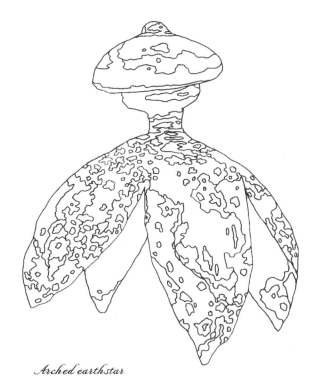

Arched earthstar

A Puff of Smoke?

Mature common puffball mushrooms feature holes at the top that release spores when bumped by animals or hit by raindrops. The spores look like puffs of smoke as they exit the mushroom, hence its name. Mushrooms reproduce by spreading spores.

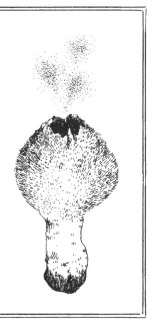

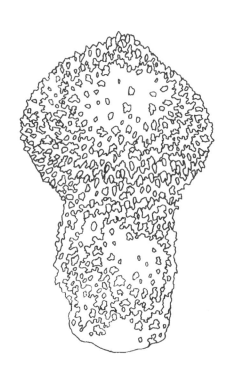

Common puffball

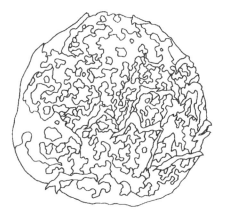

Yellow false truffle

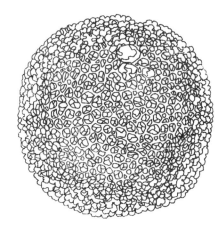

Common earthball

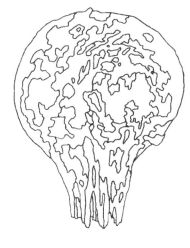

Dyeball

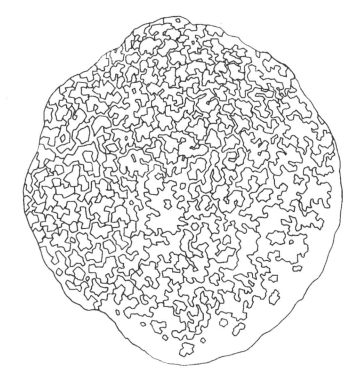

Black truffle

That's One Pricey Fungi!

Truffles are beloved among gourmet food enthusiasts, but they can cost thousands of dollars per pound! Truffles are very rare and grow underground, so pigs and dogs are used to find them.

White truffle

The Life Cycle of a Fern

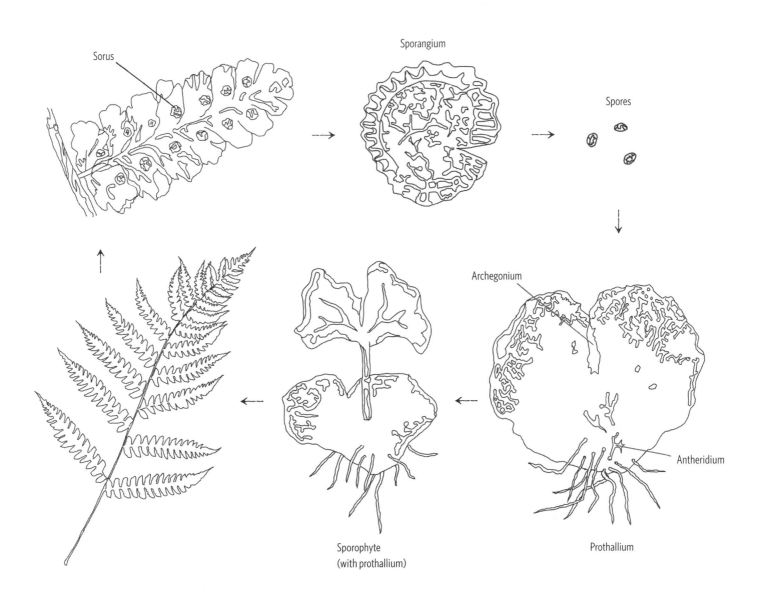

Sorus

Sporangium

Spores

Archegonium

Antheridium

Prothallium

Sporophyte
(with prothallium)

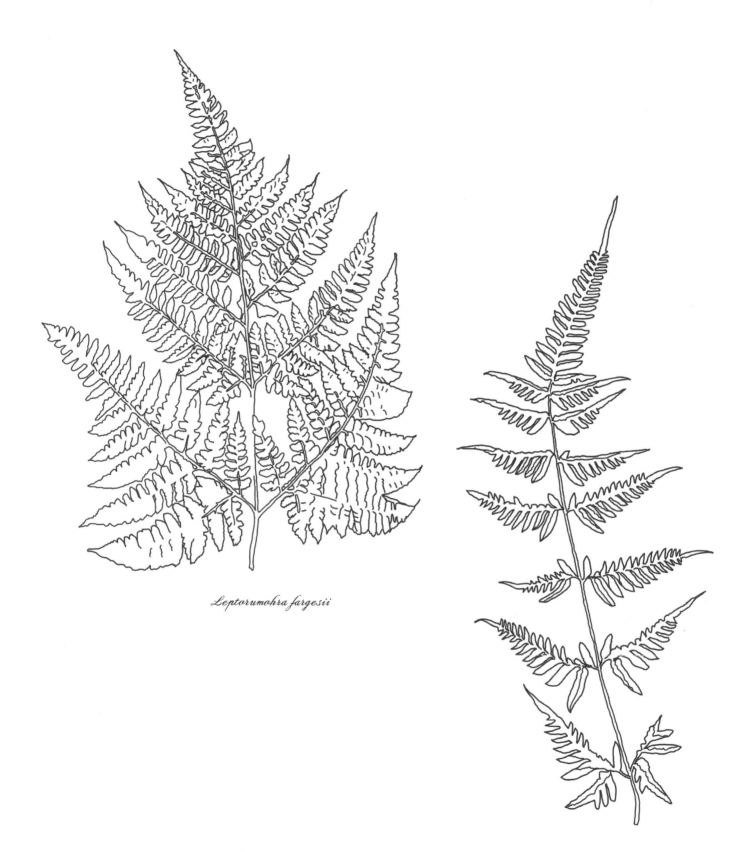

Leptorumohra fargesii

Pteris dispar

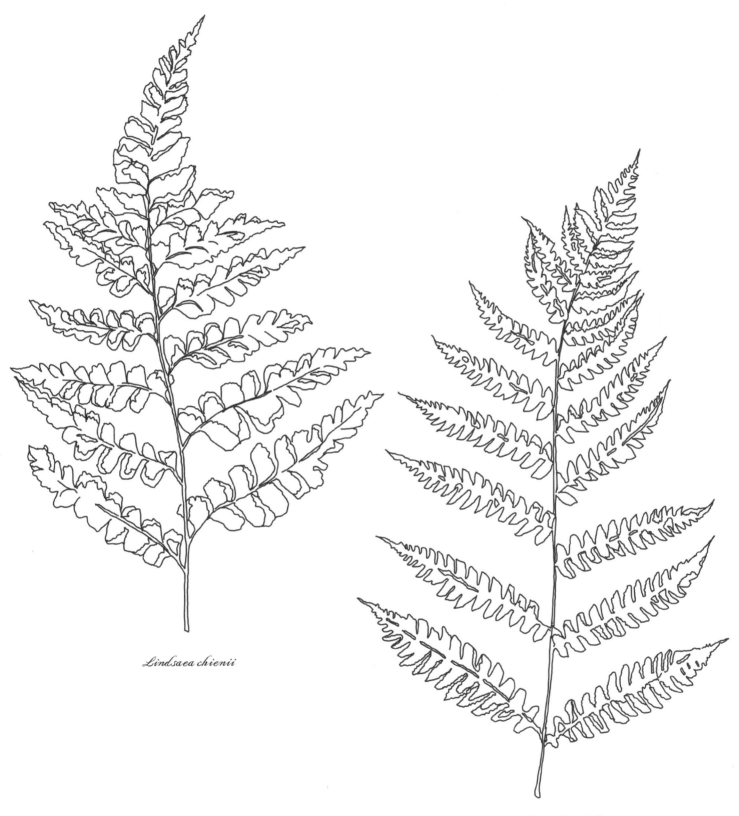

Lindsaea chienii

Deparia dimorphophylla

Bamboo-leaf oak

Ring-cupped oak

Japanese evergreen oak

Red-bark oak

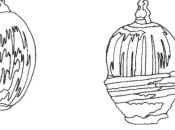

Cloud-mountain
evergreen oak

Long-leaf oak

Black ridge oak

Japanese willowleaf
oak

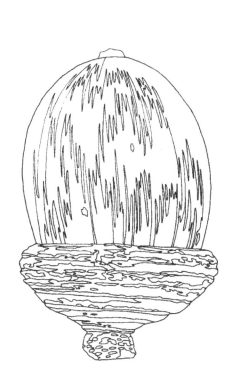

Quercus miyagii

 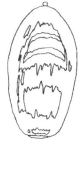

Japanese oak

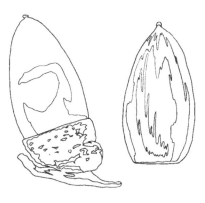

Japanese stone oak

Itaji chinkapin

Japanese chinkapin

Anatomy of an Acorn

Bottom view

Nut
A nut is basically a fruit with a hard shell

Cupule
This is like an acorn's hat!

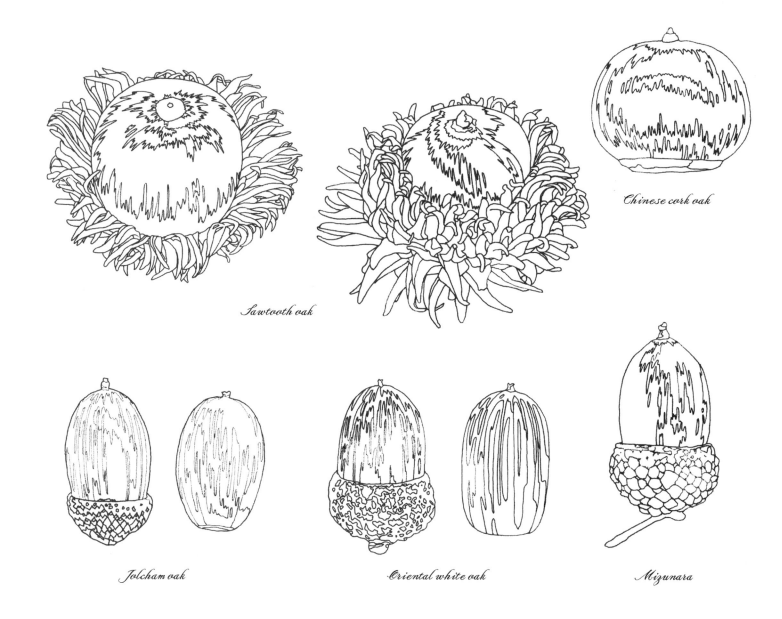

Sawtooth oak

Chinese cork oak

Jolcham oak

Oriental white oak

Mizunara

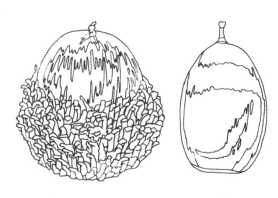

Japanese emperor oak

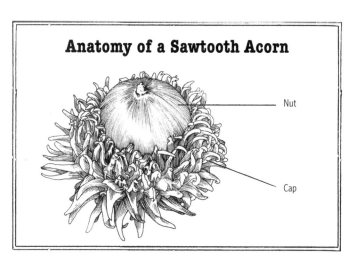

Anatomy of a Sawtooth Acorn

Nut

Cap

Tropical white oak

Black oak

Northern red oak

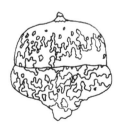

Water oak

Pin oak

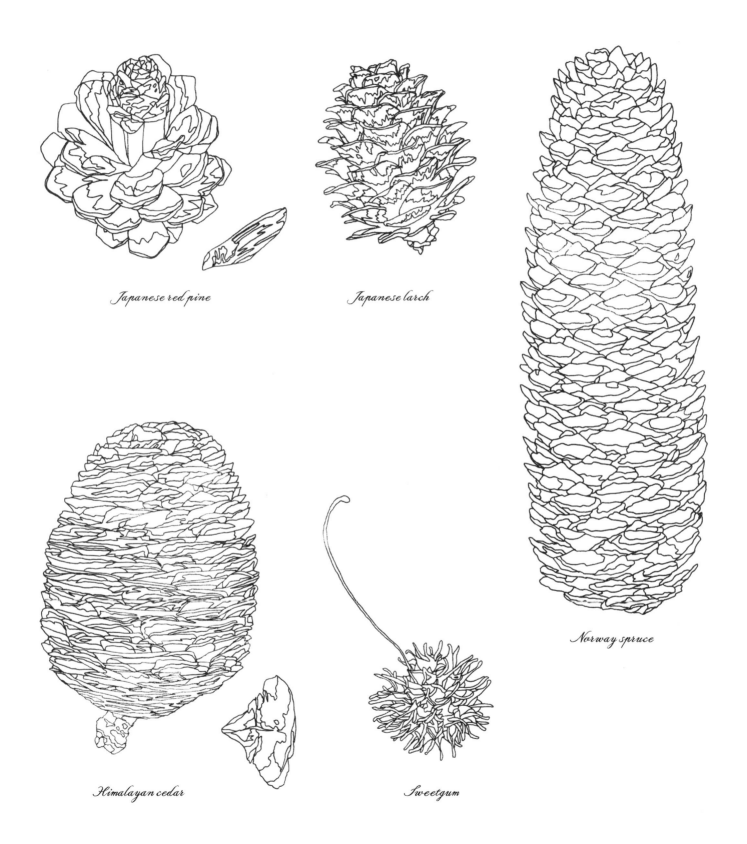

Japanese red pine

Japanese larch

Norway spruce

Himalayan cedar

Sweetgum

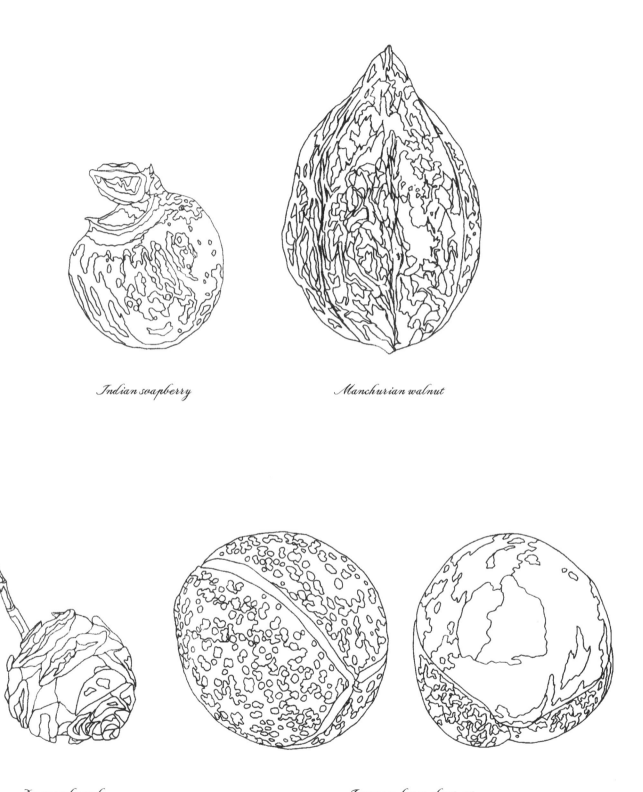

Indian soapberry

Manchurian walnut

Dawn redwood

Japanese horse chestnut

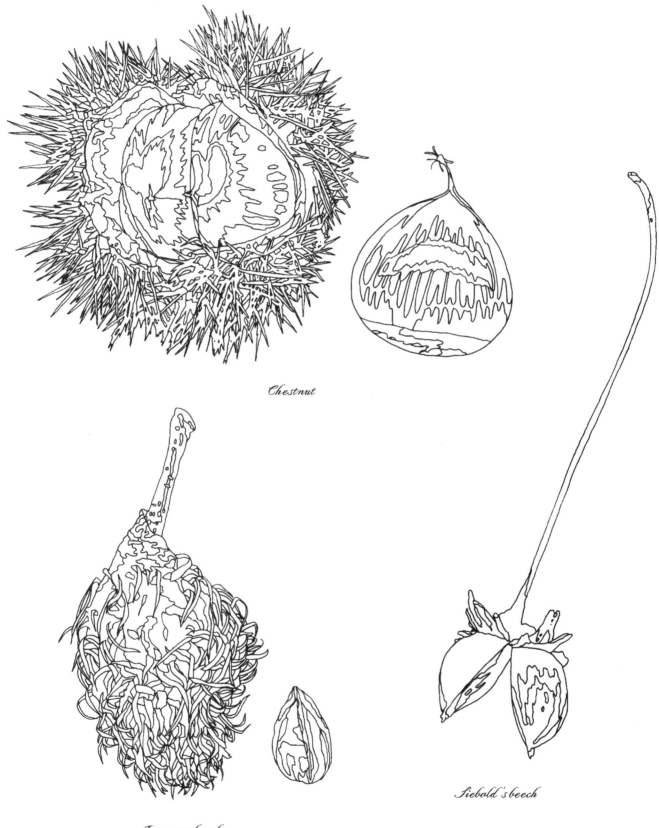

Chestnut

Japanese beech

Siebold's beech

Chinese bayberry

European blackberry

Loquat

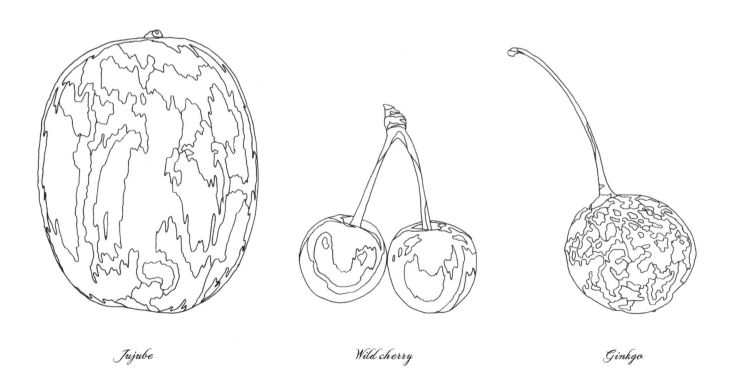

Jujube

Wild cherry

Ginkgo

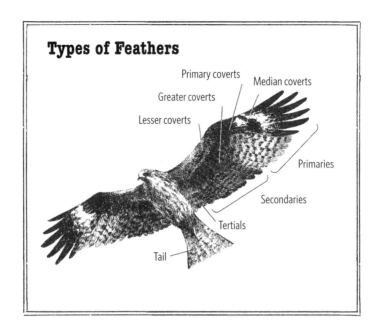

Types of Feathers

Primary coverts

Median coverts

Greater coverts

Lesser coverts

Primaries

Secondaries

Tertials

Tail

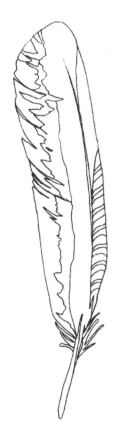

*Eurasian jay
secondary feather*

*Blue-and-white flycatcher
tail feather*

*Zitting cisticola
tail feather*

*Goldcrest
secondary feather*

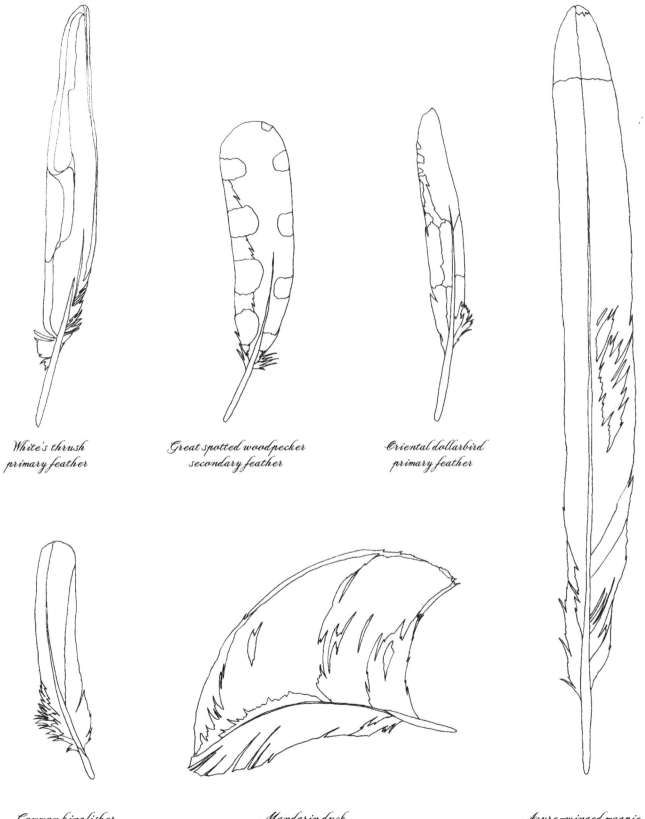

White's thrush
primary feather

Great spotted woodpecker
secondary feather

Oriental dollarbird
primary feather

Common kingfisher
secondary feather

Mandarin duck
tertial feather

Azure-winged magpie
tail feather

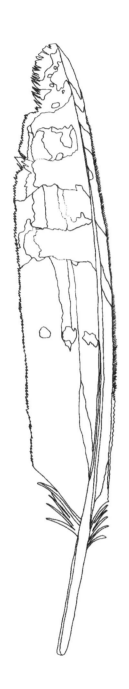

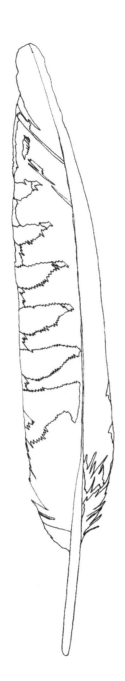

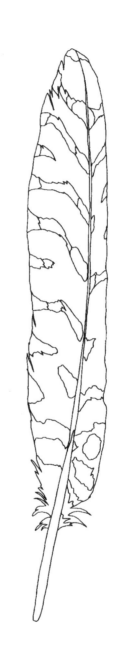

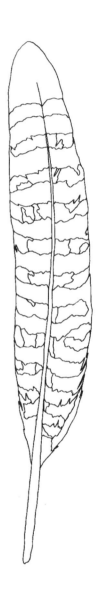

*Long-eared owl
wing feather*

*Lesser cuckoo
wing feather*

*Common cuckoo
tail feather*

*Common kestrel
tail feather*

Ural owl
wing feather

Ural owl
wing feather

Black-headed gull
wing feather

Japanese night heron
wing feather

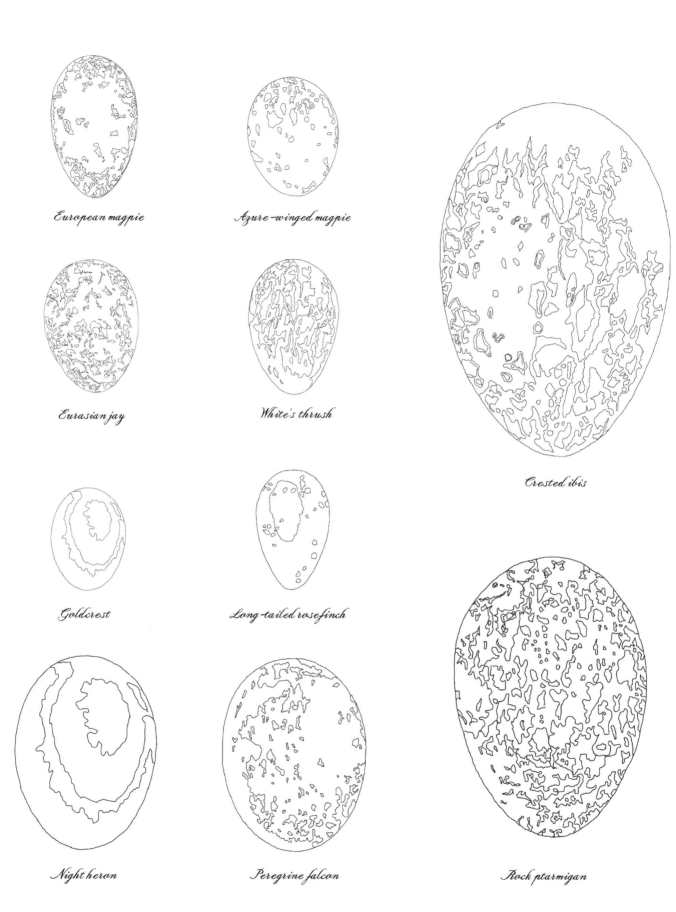

European magpie

Azure-winged magpie

Eurasian jay

White's thrush

Crested ibis

Goldcrest

Long-tailed rosefinch

Night heron

Peregrine falcon

Rock ptarmigan

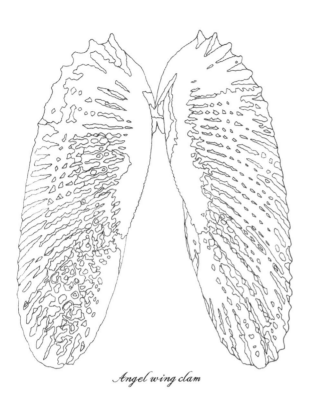

Angel wing clam

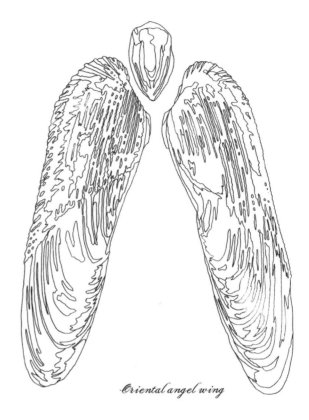

Oriental angel wing

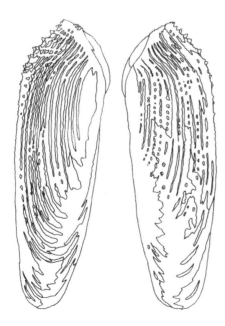

Manila piddock

Heart cockle

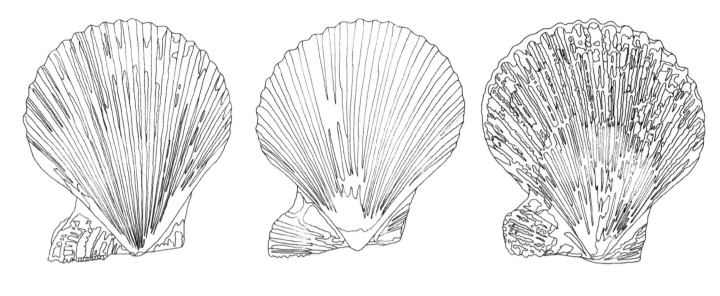

Noble scallop

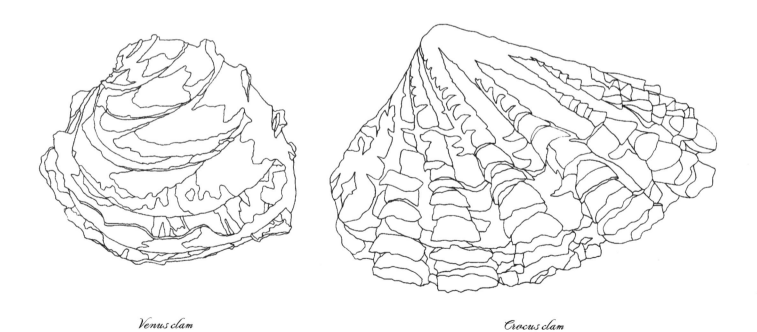

Venus clam

Crocus clam

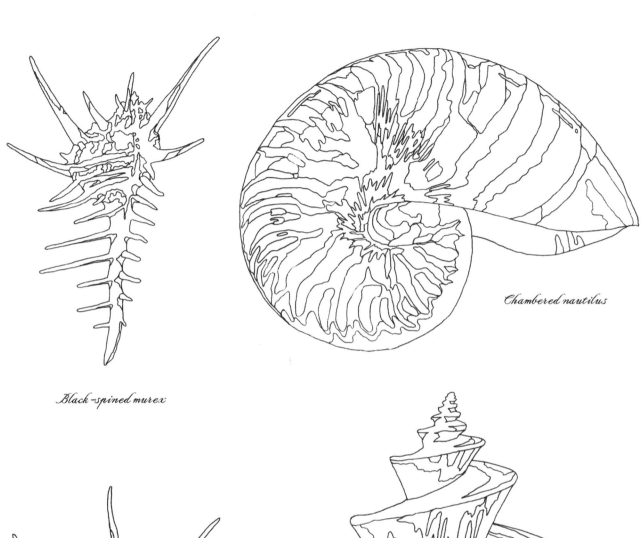

Chambered nautilus

Black-spined murex

Yoka star turban

Japanese wonder shell

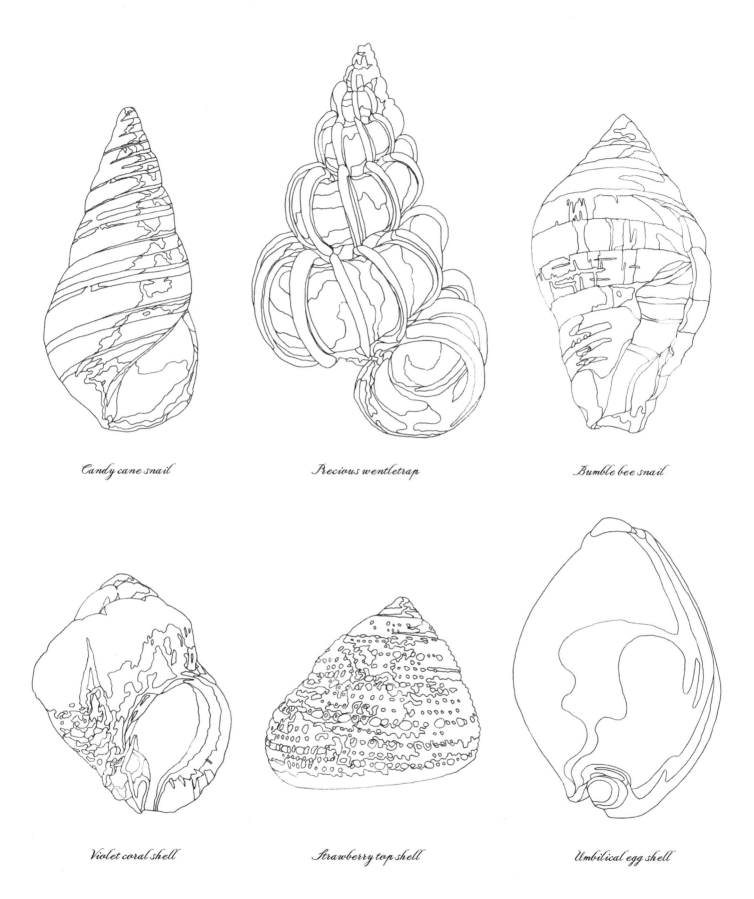

Candy cane snail

Precious wentletrap

Bumble bee snail

Violet coral shell

Strawberry top shell

Umbilical egg shell

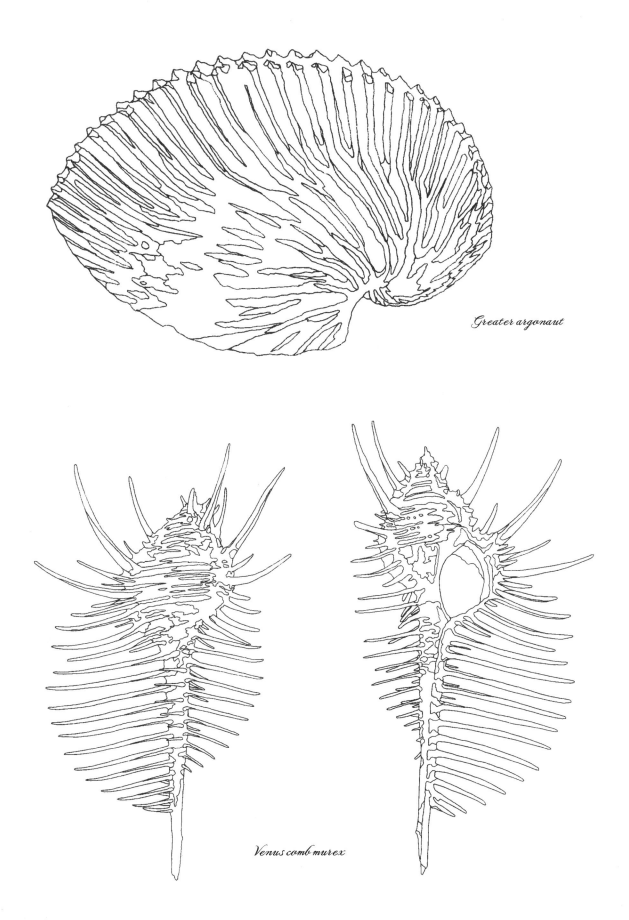

Greater argonaut

Venus comb murex

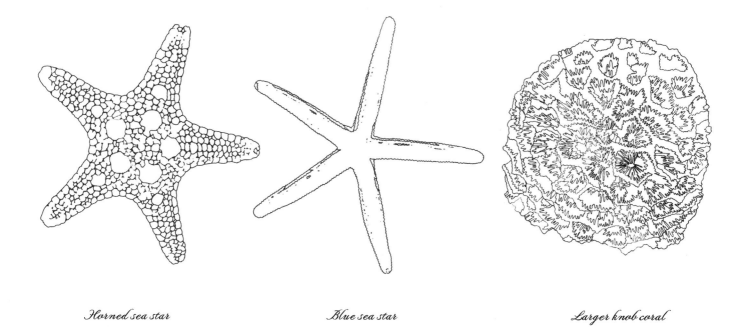

Horned sea star   *Blue sea star*   *Larger knob coral*

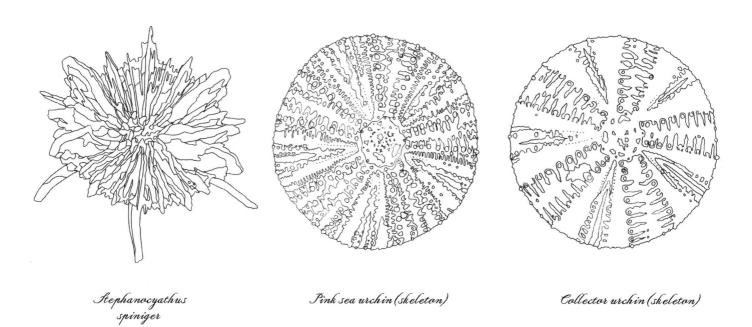

Stephanocyathus   *Pink sea urchin (skeleton)*   *Collector urchin (skeleton)*
spiniger

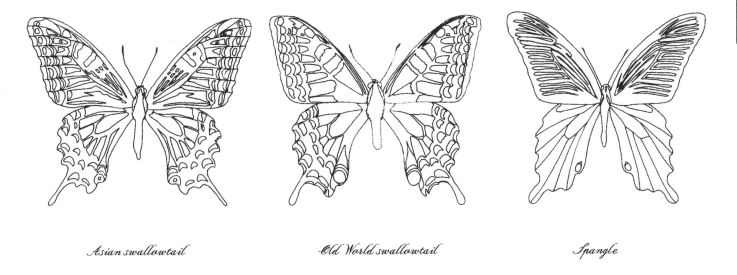

Asian swallowtail   *Old World swallowtail*   *Spangle*

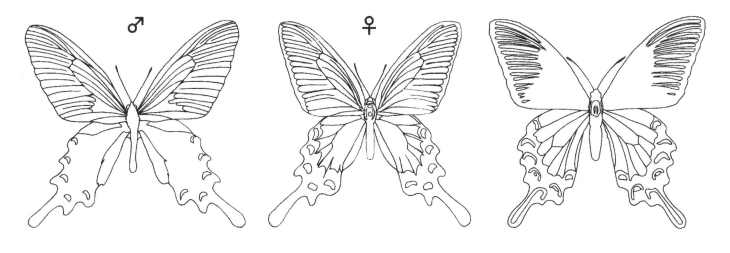

♂   ♀

Chinese windmill   *Chinese peacock*

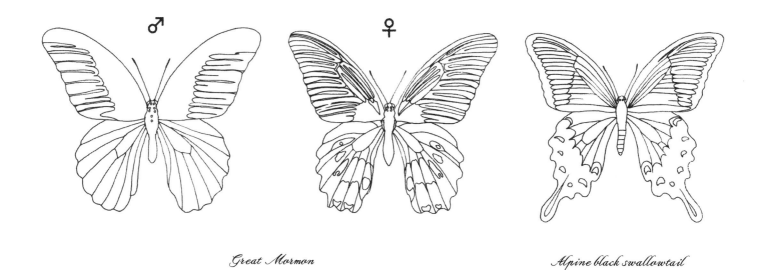

♂ ♀

Great Mormon   Alpine black swallowtail

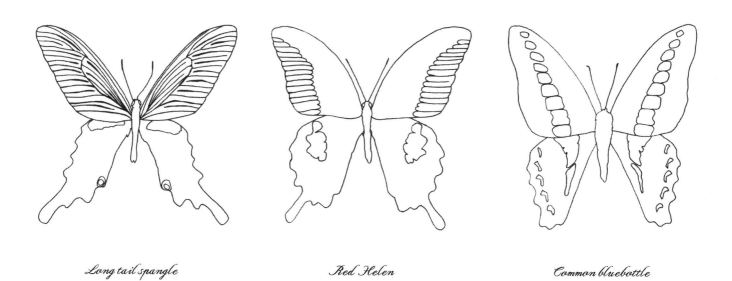

Long tail spangle   Red Helen   Common bluebottle

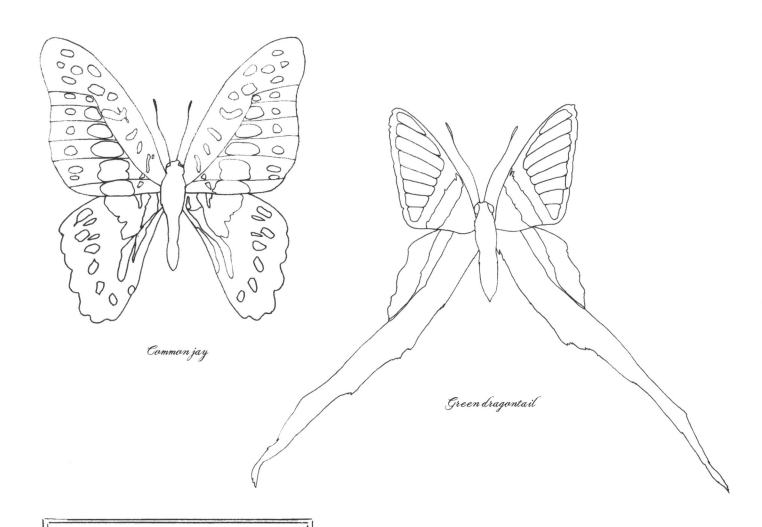

Common jay

Green dragontail

Lime butterfly

Are Those Tails?

Swallowtails are a family of large, brightly
colored butterflies. Most (but not all) species
in this family feature tails on their hind wings.
Some species, like the lime butterfly shown
above do not possess the tails.

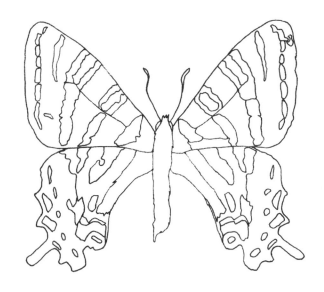

Japanese luehdorfia

Large shijimi blue   Scarce large blue   Pale grass blue

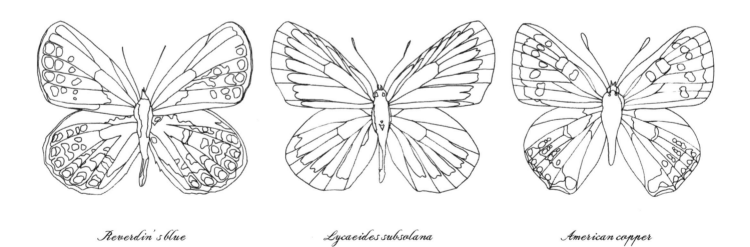

Reverdin's blue   Lycaeides subsolana   American copper

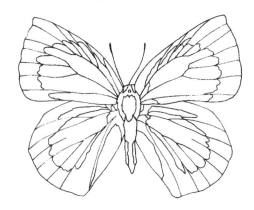

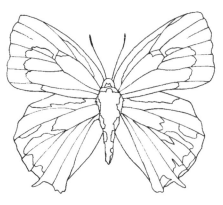

Japanese oakblue

Powdered oakblue

Short-tailed blue

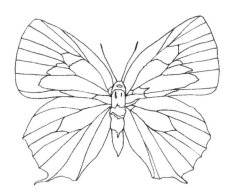

Callophrys ferrea

Neozephyrus japonicus

Wagimo signatus

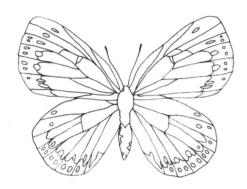

Artopoetes pryeri

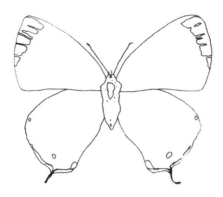

Japonica lutea

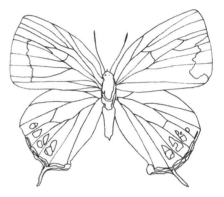

Antigius attilia

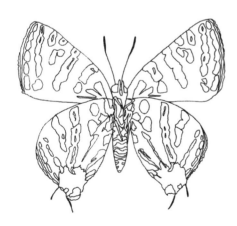

Spindasis takanonis

Araragi enthea

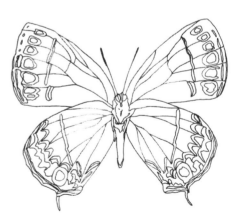

Tratsume orsedice

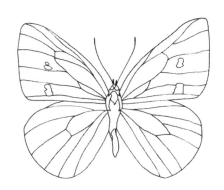

Cabbage white

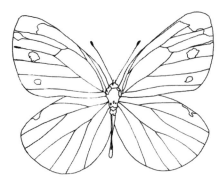

Asian green-veined white

Northeast-Asian wood white

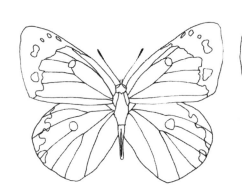

Eastern pale clouded yellow

Common grass yellow

Great orange-tip

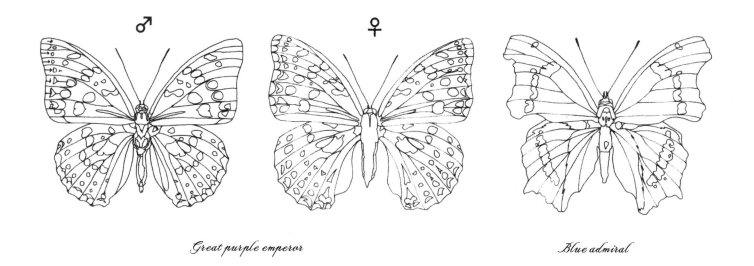

♂ ♀

Great purple emperor

Blue admiral

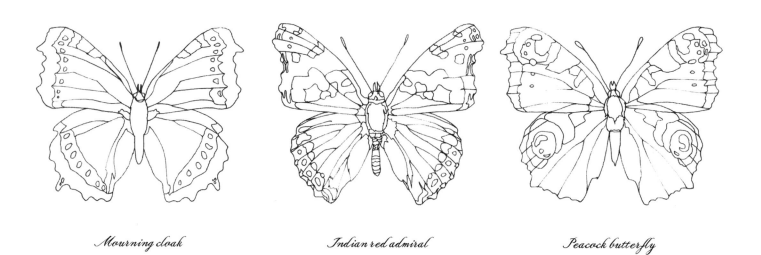

Mourning cloak

Indian red admiral

Peacock butterfly

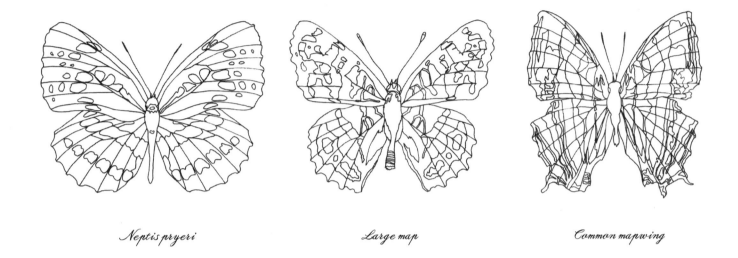

Neptis pryeri   *Large map*   *Common mapwing*

Front   *Back*

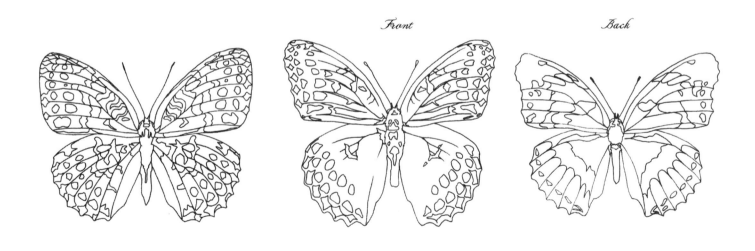

Marbled fritillary   *Damora sagana*

Asian comma

Comma

Compton tortoiseshell

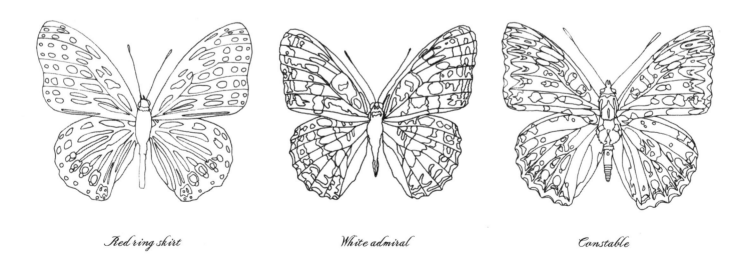

Red ring skirt

White admiral

Constable

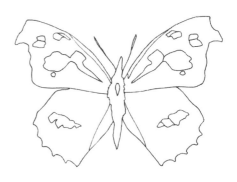

Chestnut tiger

Large tree nymph

Nettle tree butterfly

What's the Difference Between a Butterfly and a Moth?

Although there are exceptions to these rules, there are a few main differences between butteflies and moths. Butterflies display more brilliant colors, while moths are usually a drab beige or brown. This may be due in part to the fact that butterflies are active during the day, while moths are nocturnal and camouflage with bark and leaves during the daytime.

Another major difference is that butterflies fold their wings back to rest, while moths flatten their wings against their bodies.

Menelaus blue morpho

Giant blue morpho

Anaxibia morpho

Cypris morpho

Scarce morpho

Morpho rhetenor cacica

Adonis morpho

Godart's morpho

Morpho telemachus

Granada morpho

Rhetenor blue morpho

Helena morpho

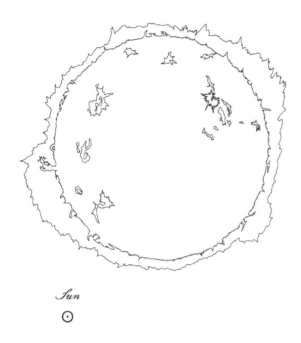

Sun

☉

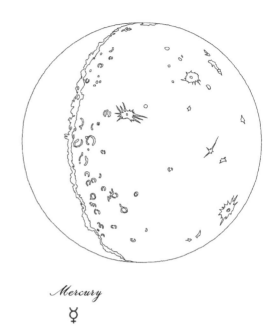

Mercury

☿

Jupiter

♃

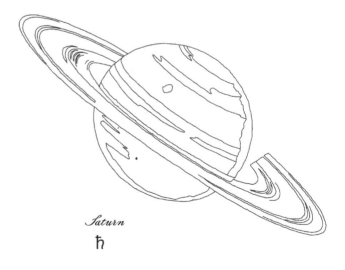

Saturn

♄

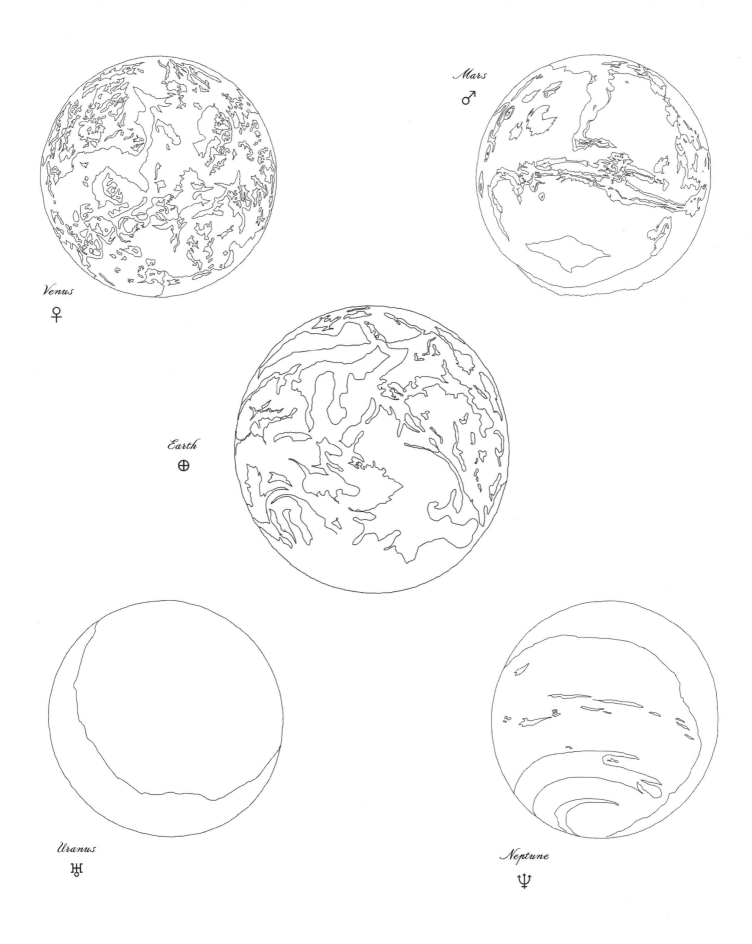

Mars
♂

Venus
♀

Earth
⊕

Uranus
♅

Neptune
♆

About the Authors

Ruchka is a collaboration between Kayoko Sato and Satoko Sasaki. The word "ruchka" means "pen" in Russian.

Kayoko Sato is the owner of Kirarasha, a shop that sells mineral specimens and other science-related goods. The shop also includes a café and holds various science workshops. Kayoko Sato previously worked as an elementary school teacher. She loves performing experiments and reading about science. Visit her website at kirara-sha.com and follow her on Instagram @cafesaya.

Satoko Sasaki is an artist who works under the name Sasakisa. She specializes in manga and watercolor illustrations inspired by nostalgia, natural science, and fantasy. Visit her website at junk-club.net and follow her on Instagram @toko_ssks.

Curious Nature Coloring Journal
First Published in 2023 by Zakka Workshop, a division of World Book Media, LLC

www.zakkaworkshop.com
134 Federal Street
Salem, MA 01970 USA
info@zakkaworkshop.com

KŌBUTSU TO RIKA-SHITSU NO NURI E
All rights reserved.
Copyright ©2016 Ruchka (Kayoko Sato & Satoko Sasaki)/GENKOSHA CO., Ltd
Original Japanese edition published by GENKOSHA CO., Ltd
English language rights, translation & production by World Book Media, LLC
through Tuttle-Mori Agency, Inc., Tokyo, Japan

Issuer: Hiroshi Kitahara
Editor: Toshimitsu Katsuyama
Planning and Editing: Sahoko Hyakutake

Art direction and design: Aya Onda
Photographs: Masashi Nagao
Cooperation: cafe SAYA
Proof reading: Yuko Sasaki
Editing: Maya Iwakawa, Atelier Kochi
English Editor: Lindsay Fair
Translation: Namiji Singley

ISBN: 978-1-940552-77-4

Printed in China

10 9 8 7 6 5 4 3 2 1